Treat the Root Cause of Imbalance and Disease

Dr. Yi Song

1

ISBN: 979-8-9948506-4-0 (print)

Regeneration Effect Publishing

This is Book Three of

Regeneration Effect :

Sacred Wisdom for Staying Young

BOOK 3

When a house catches fire, the wind can carry the flames, spreading destruction to everything in its path. But sometimes, fire behaves differently.

It hides. Beneath damp leaves and soil, a layer of "duff" can smolder quietly—too deprived of oxygen to ignite fully, yet too

alive to die. **It can stay there for years, even decades, waiting.** Then one day, a shift in the environment—a gust of wind, a change in moisture—feeds it just enough oxygen, and what was once a faint ember erupts into a full-blown blaze.

Imbalance in the body is like that duff fire.

It may start small, quietly smoldering beneath the surface where you can't see or feel it. There's not enough "oxygen" yet for it to become a visible illness, **but it's**

there—persisting, waiting for the right

conditions. Then something changes: a

stressful event, poor sleep, a diet shift, or even emotional strain. **Suddenly, what was hidden becomes a crisis.** That's why it's so important to recognize the early signs of imbalance—**while the fire is still smoldering and not yet burning through the house.**

In an interview with Sierra Clark, biohacker Valerie Orson shared that she was diagnosed with multiple sclerosis. She explained that even when using tools like red-light therapy, her cardiac metrics didn't always reach the desired levels, highlighting how sensitive her body is to stress. Because of her genetic predisposition, stressful events or environmental triggers can accelerate the development of symptoms, making her more prone to autoimmune flare-ups.

Despite these challenges, Valerie remains focused on addressing the **root cause** rather than just managing symptoms. Her experience shows that even when someone has genetic vulnerabilities, it is still possible to influence the trajectory of their health with conscious, proactive measures.

Essentially, if your body is predisposed to autoimmune conditions, it is likely already under stress—even if the source isn't immediately obvious. In Valerie's case, the exact triggers aren't always clear, despite her best efforts to minimize stress. This is a common pattern: **autoimmune tendencies almost always reflect underlying, ongoing physiological or emotional stress.**

Today, there are multiple tools—apps and devices—that can help track cardiac function, vagus nerve activity, inflammation, and other markers associated with long-term stress and autoimmune activation. Monitoring these metrics is important because it helps identify hidden stressors, evaluate progress, and guide interventions that address the **root cause** rather than just treating symptoms.

The body's immune system is no different. When it becomes confused or overworked, it can start producing antibodies against its own tissues—a misguided attempt to defend itself that ends up fueling inflammation instead. Chronic stress is often the spark behind this process, keeping the immune system in a constant state of alert.

Yes, some autoimmune conditions are linked to genetic predispositions, but even those connections are not destiny. **A gene may set the stage, but environment, stress, and lifestyle determine**

whether the fire ever ignites.

I've seen people with serious autoimmune conditions—multiple sclerosis, rheumatoid arthritis, lupus—move into remission through lifestyle changes and natural medicine alone.

Prevention, however, isn't a one-size-fits-all approach. It only works when it's *targeted*— when it respects your body's individual patterns of stress, metabolism, and recovery.

Healing begins when you learn to sense the smolder before it flames.

To listen closely, and act early, before the imbalance grows into a fire that's much harder to contain.

Many people are funneled into conventional Western medical treatments that rely heavily on immunosuppressive drugs. These medications can temporarily quiet symptoms, and in the moment it feels like progress. But over time, they take a toll— weakening tendons, thinning bones, wearing down joints, and leaving the immune system

less capable than before. And because the

underlying imbalance is never truly

addressed, the body keeps cycling through

flare-ups, searching for a stability it never receives.

The real issue begins much deeper.

An over-activated immune system isn't just "confused"—it's responding to disrupted internal signals. When the body starts producing certain proteins or enzymes incorrectly, the immune system misidentifies those molecules as foreign. **Instead of recognizing them as part of its own system, it treats them like invaders.**

This miscommunication is the spark, but the

root cause sits upstream: another system in the body isn't functioning as it should, priming the immune system to overreact long before symptoms appear.

For many people facing autoimmune conditions, this didn't happen overnight. **Their bodies have been carrying stress for years—often decades.** Emotional stress sustained over long periods subtly shifts hormonal rhythms, disturbs metabolic pathways, and strains detoxification systems. Slowly, the imbalance builds. What starts as burnout or emotional overload becomes physiological wear, and eventually the immune system begins sounding alarms in places where no threat exists.

When you look at it this way, autoimmune issues aren't just immune problems—they're whole-body communication problems.

They are the result of years of unprocessed

stress, unresolved internal tension, and

systems that have been pushed out of sync.

And unless those deeper patterns are

addressed, medications can only manage the

surface while the real story continues to

unfold underneath.

The early prevention

model focuses on

correcting the body's

imbalance before autoimmune conditions even arise.

The ideal time to treat imbalance is before autoimmune conditions develop. These conditions develop over a long period due to imbalances creating proteins that cause the body to generate antibodies to attack them.

If we **address the underlying cause** when the body just starts developing these malformed proteins, the body will never develop full-blown autoimmune conditions.

However, many full-blown autoimmune conditions in Western Medicine are categorized as **"conditions with unknown causes."** Why? Because there isn't a single protein or gene that can be traced to have 100% causal effects.

Since no specific cause can be found, the only treatments offered are immunosuppression.

Lady Gaga is an example of a celebrity

whose physical, emotional, and neurological

career demands manifested into profound

health consequences. Diagnosed with

fibromyalgia, a chronic pain condition often

triggered or exacerbated by trauma and prolonged stress, Gaga has spoken openly about how her body became a canvas for the pressures she endured. Fibromyalgia is not just generalized soreness—it involves widespread musculoskeletal pain, heightened sensitivity to stimuli, and fatigue that can make even simple movements exhausting.

The physical demands of her career only amplified these challenges. Performing at elite levels involves rigorous rehearsals, hours of vocal work, dancing, heavy costumes, and nonstop touring. Gaga is known for her theatrical shows and highly choreographed performances, which place tremendous strain on muscles, joints, and connective tissue. Layered on top of this is the neurological impact: sleep deprivation, constant travel, irregular schedules, and high-intensity performance stress create a nervous system that is perpetually in overdrive. Over time, this combination can sensitize the body to pain, trigger migraines,

and worsen fatigue.

But the physical toll is only part of the

story. Lady Gaga has also been candid

about living with PTSD, a condition that

keeps the nervous system hyper-alert and

amplifies physical pain. Trauma can disrupt

the body's natural healing processes,

dysregulate immune function, and create

chronic inflammation—all of which feed

into the cycle of fibromyalgia and other

stress-related conditions. In essence, her

body "held" the cumulative stress of her career, her trauma, and the demands of constant public exposure, translating invisible emotional and psychological strain into very tangible, long-term physical consequences.

Her experience demonstrates a critical point: **Even extraordinary talent, drive, and resilience cannot fully protect the body from overexertion.**

Chronic stress, physical overwork, and unprocessed trauma combine to create conditions that are difficult to reverse.

Gaga's story underscores the importance of listening to the body, respecting its limits, and integrating recovery and self-care—not as optional extras, but as essential components of sustainable health, particularly for anyone living under intense professional or public pressure.

I once saw a cartoon in the newspaper. A cat meets a dog and says:

"You have four legs and a tail. I have four legs and a tail.

Therefore, you must be a cat."

It's a perfect illustration of a false analogy—

mistaking similarity for sameness. We can

see the logic error instantly in the cartoon,

but when it comes to our health, we fall for

it all the time. **Two conditions might share

similar symptoms—fatigue, weight gain,

brain fog—but that doesn't mean they

share the same root cause.**

Without someone who can tell which of

your "symptoms are cats" and which are

"dogs," you can spend years chasing the

wrong diagnosis. My friend Bruce did

exactly that. He tried everything most people try. He invested in the latest gadgets, ran countless functional medicine tests, and experimented with every diet that promised results. He even considered celebrity-level protocols, but as he said, "I could follow them, but it'll cost thousands of dollars, and I'm not sure it will work."

In hindsight, he realized that his fragmented approach—jumping from one test, supplement, or trend to another—only added to his stress. Each "solution" addressed one piece of the puzzle but ignored the whole picture.

Over time, those accumulated stresses, combined with years of overwork and self-imposed pressure, began to take a toll.

His biggest mistake wasn't a single bad habit—it was underestimating how much chronic stress could silently erode his health.

Eventually, his body began to send louder signals, until one specialist finally uncovered the real issue: a rare autoimmune disorder.

That moment was a turning point.

Everything suddenly made sense—the exhaustion, the stubborn weight, the constant feeling of being "off." Bruce realized that if he had focused on early prevention, managing his stress, and understanding his body's unique needs instead of chasing quick fixes, he might have avoided years of frustration and decline.

That small detail, can completely change

how your body responds.

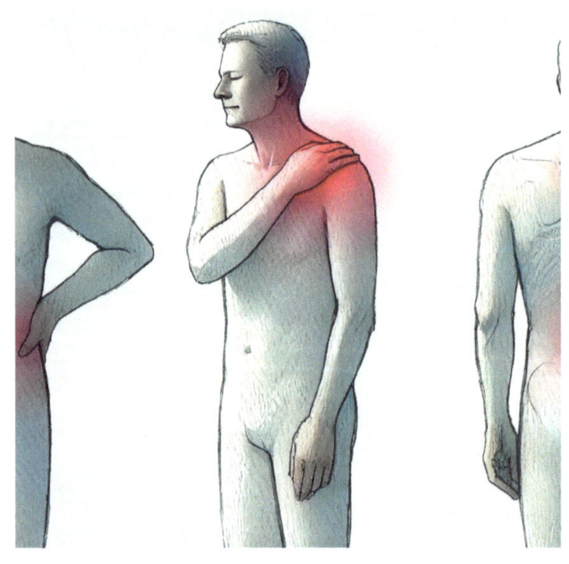

In Chinese medicine, this concept is

foundational: *treat disease before it*

appears.

Too many people are hacking the symptoms without ever addressing the root causes.

If your sleep is poor, your diet is inflammatory, and your stress is unchecked, no amount of red-light therapy or cryotherapy will save you. It'll be like trying to upgrade a software system on a computer with a broken hard drive.

Sometimes people suddenly lose their hearing—maybe after an acute inflammation, a viral infection, a dive, or even just a pressure change on a plane. Often, tinnitus shows up right alongside it. The typical Western response is a steroid injection. It can reduce inflammation, but it focuses on

symptoms rather than the deeper issue.

Tinnitus usually involves the inner ear and the nerve pathways that carry sound signals to the brain. To genuinely address the root cause, you have to support and repair the inner ear itself.

And that's where Chinese medicine has a real advantage.

Western medicine doesn't have many tools for regenerating or strengthening the inner ear, but **herbal formulas, acupuncture, and circulation-boosting therapies can make a big difference**—especially when treatment starts early. The best window is right when the condition begins, before steroids or prednisone. These medications help some people, but for many others they don't do enough, and the issue becomes chronic.

The earlier you respond, the easier the solution—and the less damage done over time.

If something feels "off," don't brush it aside.

Get curious. Address it.

Your future self will thank you.

To get in-depth discussion to Treat your Root Cause of Imbalance and Disease, scan the QR code to preorder "Regeneration Effect: Sacred Wisdom for Staying Young" and learn how you can implement all the principles in your life.

ABOUT THE AUTHOR

Dr. Yi Song was born and raised in Beijing, China, into a family with seventeen generations of experience in both Chinese and Western medicine. Twenty-eight years ago, she came to the United States to study pathology at Brown University. After observing the shortcomings of symptom-focused treatments, Dr. Song returned to her roots to focus on true regenerative healing — addressing disease at its source. She has had a holistic clinic in Boston since 2004. In 2018, she founded the Zenerchi Retreat in

Medellin, Colombia. Her introduction to stem cell therapy in 2020 was marked by her mother's successful treatment and subsequent independence at age 81. Dr. Song believes that stem cell therapy aligns with holistic principles and is the author of "Regeneration Effect: Sacred Wisdom for Staying Young" and the series of seven books in "The Six Principles to Natural Longevity". Her vision is to combine stem cell therapy, Traditional Chinese Medicine, and anti-aging treatments to help people live a long, high-quality life. She offers advanced stem cell treatments at Zenerchi Retreat in Colombia not available in the US. You can also get consultation about your conditions and concerns in person in Boston or at our network of doctors in the US and online.